Royal Geographical Society Exploring Series

EXPLORING AUSTRALIA

Ian Cameron

Longman

Contents

Royal Geographical Society

Exploring Australia has been written with the help of the Royal Geographical Society. This Society has been working for more than 150 years "for the promotion of that most important and entertaining branch of knowledge, geography." In the past it sponsored many of the world's great explorers – Livingstone in Africa, Scott and Shackleton in the Antarctic, Hillary and Tenzing on Everest. Today it is busier than ever. It has the world's largest private collection of maps, and a magnificent library; its publications and lectures play a leading role in geographical teaching and research; more than 100 expeditions apply to it annually for help, and each year it sends large numbers of explorers, research-workers, scientists and conservationists to the farthest ends of the Earth.

I should like to thank the Royal Geographical Society very much indeed for their support and encouragement, for allowing me the use of their library, map-room and archives, and for providing most of the book's illustrations.

Ian Cameron

Cover: The desert near Alice Springs, Northern Territory.

Back cover: Droving in the Northern Territory.

Endpapers: The Olgas, west of Ayers Rock, Northern Territory.

Title spread: Sydney Harbour, painted by Thomas Baines, 1857.

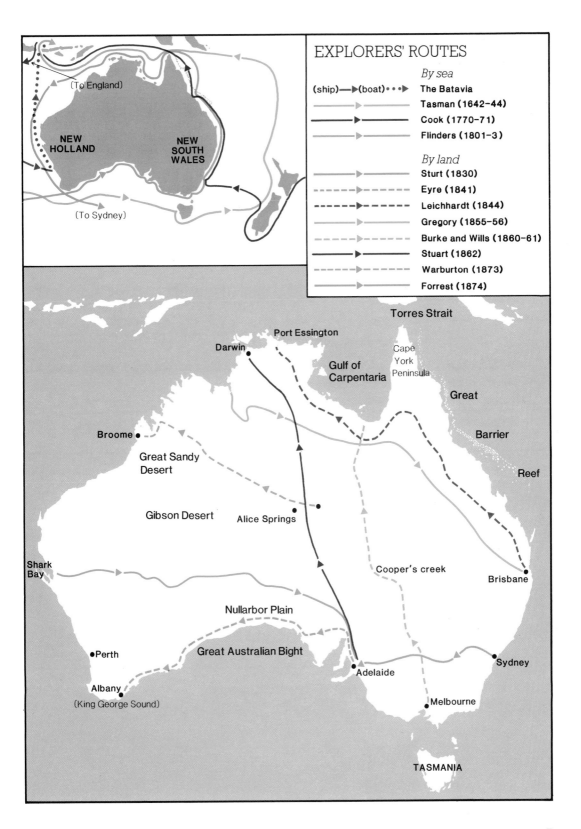

EXPLORERS' ROUTES

By sea

(ship) ▶ (boat) • • ▶   The Batavia

Tasman (1642–44)

Cook (1770–71)

Flinders (1801–3)

By land

Sturt (1830)

Eyre (1841)

Leichhardt (1844)

Gregory (1855–56)

Burke and Wills (1860–61)

Stuart (1862)

Warburton (1873)

Forrest (1874)

(To England)

NEW HOLLAND

NEW SOUTH WALES

(To Sydney)

Torres Strait

Port Essington

Darwin

Cape York Peninsula

Gulf of Carpentaria

Great

Barrier

Reef

Broome

Great Sandy Desert

Gibson Desert

Alice Springs

Shark Bay

Cooper's creek

Brisbane

Nullarbor Plain

Great Australian Bight

Perth

Adelaide

Sydney

Albany (King George Sound)

Melbourne

TASMANIA

7

Australia: The Awakening Giant

Area: 7,695,064 square kilometres

Mean elevation: 305 metres

Highest point: 2,230 metres (Mount Kosciusko, NSW)

Highest recorded temperature: 40·6°C (Cloncurry, Queensland))

Lowest recorded temperature: −15·0°C (Kiandra, NSW).

The name Australia comes from the Latin word *australis*, meaning southern.

Terra Australis Incognita (the Unknown Southern Land) was the name given by ancient geographers to the huge landmass which, they believed, must surely exist in the southern hemisphere to balance the huge landmass of Eurasia in the northern hemisphere. For it was thought in those days that the world must be symmetrical and balanced. It was a long time before people realised that although most of the northern hemisphere is land, most of the southern hemisphere is sea; the world is not symmetrical at all; the *Terra Australis* of the ancients was a myth . . .

When the Dutch first sighted the west coast of the continent we now call Australia, they named it New Holland. When the British first sighted the east coast they named it New South Wales. Some people wondered if New Holland and New South Wales might perhaps be separate islands. However, in 1802/3 Matthew Flinders sailed all the way round the continent, and proved that it was one continuous landmass. So it was Flinders who put Australia accurately on the world map. And it was Flinders who gave it its name. For after his voyage he wrote: *"Now that New Holland and New South Wales are known to form one land, there must be a general name* (given) *to the*

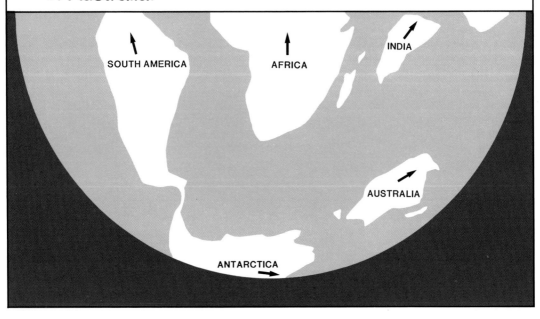

The Southern Hemisphere in the Cretaceous Era, about 60 million years ago, showing the isolation of Australia.

whole, and I have ventured to re-adopt the original name *Terra Australis.* Had I permitted myself any change it would have been to convert *Australis* to *Australia.*"

*   *   *

The early European explorers of Australia nearly all describe the continent as "strange". On its trees the leaves hung upside-down, "not so much evergreen as evergrey". In its deserts were giant birds which never flew, and strange animals which hopped rather than walked. Its swans were not white but black. Why, they wondered, was everything so different?

Australia is different from other continents because it has evolved in a different way: in isolation.

Geologists tell us that about 90 million years ago the Earth consisted of two super-continents: Laurasia in the northern hemisphere, and Gondwanaland in the southern. In the north the continents remained relatively stationary and close to one another: plants, animals and people were therefore able to move freely from one landmass to the next. In the south, on the other hand, the continents were relatively mobile and became widely separated. India moved northwards, right across the equator, and collided with Asia. Africa moved northward and collided with Europe. South America attached itself to North America. Australia and Antarctica were then left to drift in isolation around the South Pole. Eventually Australia became detached and began to move into roughly its present position. The map on page 8 shows the continent as it probably was about 50 million years ago.

It was isolated then. It has remained isolated ever since. Few animals have migrated to it from other lands; few seeds have been washed on to it from other continents. Its plants and animals were therefore able to evolve a life-style specially suited to Australian conditions, and to develop in their own distinctive way. An

Above: An Aborigine in Queensland, painted by Thomas Baines in 1855.

Below: Aborigines in Western Australia preparing for a ceremony.

example is the kangaroo, which is unlike any other animal in any other continent.

What is true of Australia's plants and animals is true also of its people.

Over the last 25,000 years it seems probable that there have been only three small migrations into Australia. In about 20,000 BC a short, stocky, dark-skinned people, the Negritos, made their way across the shallow seas from New Guinea and settled along the north coast. They were followed, some 5,000 years later, by a people with lighter skins and possibly greater intelligence. These were the Murrayians, who almost certainly came from the Philippines. Then, after roughly another 5,000 years, came the Carpentarians: a people with light-brown skin, straight hair and almost Nordic features. They came from India. These three races intermingled to form the Aborigines.

Left to their own devices for thousands of years, the Aborigines evolved a way-of-life which was peaceful and well-suited to the land

Australia's varied terrain. Left: the plains. Right: the desert. Opposite: The rain forest.

in which they lived. They became nomads, who hunted animals and gathered fruit and seeds for food. They formed into small tribal units, which were tied by both economic necessity and religious belief to a particular area of land. It used to be fashionable to describe the Aborigines as "primitives"; and it is certainly true that they grew no crops, kept no livestock, built no cities and had almost no material possessions. But it is also true that they had no wars, that their children hardly ever cried, and that their old and their sick were loved and cared for. Their culture was already old when Tutankhamen was buried in his pyramid; and in many ways they were a more attractive people than the acquisitive Europeans who were about to rob them of the land which meant so much to them.

The first of these Europeans to arrive off Australia may have been Portuguese. However, Portuguese sightings of Australia are conjecture, not fact. There was a map published in France in 1544 which *may* have been drawn from Portuguese charts. This map shows a coastline called *Jave le Grande* running south from Indonesia, which *may* represent Australia. Also a pair of cannons recently unearthed from Broome Bay *may* have been made in Lisbon in about 1550. While an engraving published in Portugal at much the same time *may* show an animal with young in its pouch which could be a kangaroo. All this makes it probable – but by no means certain – that the first Europeans to sight Australia were the Portuguese.

After the Portuguese came the Spaniards; and their first sighting is better documented. In August, 1606 two ships, *San Pedrico* and *Los Tres Reyes*, commanded by Luis de Torres, entered the narrow strait between Australia and New Guinea. They sighted land to the south, and anchored off "a very large island" where they saw people "black-skinned and altogether naked". The fact that Torres describes the people as "black-skinned and altogether naked" gives us a clue to their identity; for both before and after this sighting he describes the people of New Guinea as "not very white, and naked except for their private parts". In other words the people he saw on the island were *not* natives of New Guinea. They must therefore have been Aborigines. The place where they were sighted was almost certainly Banks Island off the tip of the Cape York Peninsula.

These sightings by the Portuguese and the Spaniards were followed almost immediately by landings by the Dutch.

1 The First Landings

There was a full moon off the coast of west Australia and the *Batavia* was sailing fast. A full moon, a fair wind and a scattering of cloud, so that the sea was here dark and there dappled with patches of moonlight. The captain of the *Batavia*, Ariaen Jacobsz, was on deck, and he pointed anxiously to a whitening of the sea ahead. "It's all right," he was told, "it's only moonshine."

A moment later the *Batavia* struck a reef.

The ship heeled over with a terrible splintering crash, and came to rest impaled on the jagged rocks. Passengers and crew, as they scrambled up from below, were greeted by spray flung high over their mast and waves sluicing green the length of the deck. "God have mercy", one of them whispered, "on our souls". Seldom was a prayer more heartfelt or more needed; because for the *Batavia's* 300 passengers and crew the wreck of their ship was only the first and the least terrible of the disasters about to engulf them . . .

The *Batavia*, flagship of the Dutch East India fleet, had run aground in June 1629 on the Abrolhos, a chain of low islands and half-submerged reefs some 400 kilometres to the north of Perth.

Neither the west coast nor the north coast of Australia was a happy hunting-ground for the Dutch. Dutch seamen sighted the Australian coast many times during the first half of the 17th century, and charted parts of it with some accuracy. They called the country they had discovered New Holland, after their homeland. Yet they made no effort to land on it and explore it. And if one asks why, the answer seems to lie partly in the character of the coast of Australia and partly in the character of the Dutch.

Australia's northern and western coasts are for the most part bleak and difficult to land on.

The north coast is often choked with mangrove swamps, and its inshore waters are too shallow to be safe for sailing. The west coast is barren; also it is a lee shore – that is to say the prevailing wind blows straight on to it from the sea – and such a shore was (and still is) a graveyard for sailing ships. In the 6,500-odd kilometres of coastline between the Great Australian Bight in the south and the Gulf of Carpentaria in the north there are few good harbours. But even if there *had* been good harbours it is doubtful if the Dutch would have used them. For Australia didn't offer them what they were looking for. The 17th century Dutch were traders not settlers. They didn't want to found colonies, but to find commodities: commodities which would fetch a high price in the markets of Europe. In particular they were looking for spices (nutmeg, mace, cinnamon, cloves and, above all, pepper) and gold. Australia had no spices, and to outward appearances no gold. The Dutch were therefore disappointed in the continent. They described it as "worthless", and its inhabitants as "miserable". The only use they had for it was as a landfall, a turning point in their voyages to their busy trading ports in Indonesia, which was known in those days as the Dutch East Indies.

In 1611 the Dutch captain Hendrik Brouwer had discovered that by sailing first due east and then due north from Cape Town a ship could avoid being becalmed in the doldrums of the Indian Ocean and could pick up favourable winds and currents for the whole journey to Indonesia. All Dutch captains were ordered to follow this new route. The trouble was that seamen in those days couldn't judge accurately how far they had sailed. So many ships – like the *Batavia* – headed east for too long and were brought up short by the coast of Australia.

We know from Dutch East India Company records and from the logs of Dutch East India-men that the west coast of Australia was sighted many times during the early 17th century. In 1616 the *Harmony* anchored off Shark Bay. In 1618 the *Mauritius* sighted Exmouth Gulf. In 1619 the *Amsterdam* made a landfall near present-day Perth – "we could find no place to put ashore", wrote her captain, "because of the heavy surf." In 1622 the *Lioness*

Dutch East Indiamen, 1726, off Rottnest Island, Western Australia. The black swans prominently featured.

sighted the great storm-lashed headland that forms the southwestern tip of Australia; and a few years later the *Golden Seahorse* sailed right round this headland into the Great Australian Bight. These were important discoveries. Yet the Dutch seldom landed and never settled. Indeed it is doubtful, in these early years, if a Dutch ship's company ever *voluntarily* spent the night on Australian soil. It was a different story *involuntarily . . .*

Soon after running aground on the Abrolhos the *Batavia* broke up.

If passengers and crew had worked together they might have saved the *Batavia*. However, some of the crew were intent on saving themselves. Others were intent on loot – even before the ship was wrecked, mutineers were planning to seize it – and the passengers lacked a leader. So when the *Batavia* was finally battered to destruction, there was confusion. Some passengers found temporary shelter on one of the tiny Abrolhos islands. Some mutineers found shelter on another island. Most of the crew, led by François Pelsaert (an officer of the Dutch East India Company) set out in the ship's boat to seek help from Java. It took Pelsaert a month to reach Java, and nearly as long to return with a rescue ship. And what a terrible scene he came back to!

In the two months he had been away, the mutineers had seized the *Batavia*'s cargo and murdered, with appalling brutality, more than 120 of the passengers. The mutineers murder-

Above: The black swans of Western Australia (with white cygnets) which must have so astonished the European explorers.

Right: A contemporary portrait of Captain Cook, painted by Webber, and a contemporary engraving of his ship Endeavour *beached for repairs after being holed on the Great Barrier Reef.*

ed the passengers who refused to join them in cold blood and without the slightest remorse . . . *"Jonas was ordered to go with Zeevanck and others to Seal's Island, and kill the 4 women and 15 boys who had avoided death in the previous massacre . . . So Jonas went up to Mayken Soers who was pregnant, and took her by the hand and said 'Now Mayken, my dear, you must die'; then he flung her to the ground and cut her throat. Having done this, he saw that another man was having difficulty killing Janneken Gist, so he went to help, and stabbed Janneken to death with his knife. The two remaining women and the young boys were then killed by the others."* This was followed by the murder of Vrouwe Bastiansz and her six children, including an 18-month-old baby. Some of the men-passengers were given the option of killing their companions or being killed themselves. Some of the women-passengers were given the option of being killed or becoming the "concubines" of the mutineers. In all the annals of seafaring there is no more sickening example of inhumanity.

With the return of Pelsaert, the mutineers were rounded up and brought to justice. Some had their hands cut off and were hanged on the spot. Others were taken to Java to an even more terrible death: "to be tied in public to a wheel and their bodies broken from under upwards". Two of them, Wouter Looes and Jan Pelgrom, were marooned.

Looes and Pelgrom were given a ship's boat, "well provisoned and watered", and were set adrift near the mouth of a large river – probably Murchison. What happened to them will never be known; but they must have survived for weeks if not for months or even years. They can therefore be regarded as the first white settlers of Australia. One wonders what the gentle Aborigines must have thought of them?

*　　*　　*

There was bright moonlight off the coast of east Australia, and the *Endeavour*, like the *Batavia* a century and a half earlier, was also sailing fast.

To quote the ship's captain, James Cook: *"11th June 1770 . . . A few minutes before 11 p.m. we had 17 fathom* (31 metres), *but before the man at the lead could (make) another cast, the ship struck and stuck fast . . . We had got upon the SE edge of a reef of coral."*

The *Endeavour* had run aground on the Great Barrier Reef, about 80 kilometres to the south of present-day Cooktown on the east coast of Australia.

British seamen didn't sight the east coast of Australia nearly as often as Dutch seamen sighted the west coast. Yet they explored it more thoroughly, *and* they settled on it. And if

Whitsunday Islands off the coast of Queensland, discovered on Whitsunday 1770 by Captain Cook.

one asks why the British took so much more interest in Australia than the Dutch, the answer would seem to lie partly in the character of the east Australian coast and partly in the character of the British.

The east coast of Australia is more inviting than the west coast. It is less arid; its prevailing wind is offshore rather than onshore, and it has more and better harbours – Sydney has been described simply as "the finest natural harbour in the world". But even if east Australia had been without harbours, the British would almost certainly have settled there. For Australia offered them what they were looking for – the opportunity to make new scientific discoveries, and the opportunity to establish strategic military bases in the southern hemi-

sphere. This dual objective is brought out very clearly in Cook's sailing orders. *"From a place southward of the Equinoctial Line you are to observe the passage of the Planet Venus over the disk of the sun . . . and to observe with accuracy such lands as you may discover, and take possession of them in the name of his Majesty."* So when, in April 1770, Cook's expedition sighted the east coast of Australia, the new-found land appeared to offer everything they could have hoped for.

Cook's first landfall in Australia was Point Hicks Hill, roughly midway between Sydney and Melbourne; and his first impression was of *"an agreeable and pleasant countrie: of hills covered in part with trees and bushes, and interspersed with tracts of sand."* He followed the coastline north until he came to Botany Bay, where he landed. In Botany Bay Cook was again impressed with the "promising Aspect of the countrie". His naturalist Joseph Banks was even more enthusiastic, describing the land as *"completely fascinating, and a veritable treasure trove of strange plants and insects"* – during a stay of less than a week Banks collected over 200 new species, all of them unknown in Europe.

Leaving Botany Bay, the *Endeavour* again headed north. The weather was fine. The country was beautiful. The sea, to Cook's surprise, became calmer and calmer. However, the calmness was deceptive. For *Endeavour* was now venturing into one of the most dangerous seaways in the world, the shallows inside the Great Barrier Reef.

Suddenly and without warning the ship struck a submerged bank of coral.

Endeavour came to rest, "shuddering horribly". Within seconds the ship was being pounded so violently by the waves that the crew could hardly keep their feet. Looking over the side they saw that part of their keel had been ripped clean away and timbers were being tossed about in the surf. The *Endeavour* was in much the same situation as the *Batavia* had been in when it struck the Abrolhos. But the reaction of the crew was very different. They fought to save her. *"No crew,"* wrote Cook, *"ever behaved better. Every man had a sence of the danger we were*

in, and exerted himself to the utmost." They lightened the ship by throwing overboard guns, ballast and even some of their food. They towed *Endeavour* off the reef, only to find that the ship had sprung so terrible a leak that the combined efforts of officers and men at the pumps couldn't stem the inrush of water. So they "fothered" the keel: that is to say they soaked a sail in wool, sheep's dung and oakum (fibrous hemp), passed it under the ship and *"hauld it by ropes from one part of the ship's bottom to another untill we found the place where it took effect."* The leak wasn't completely plugged; but the inflow of water was slowed down sufficiently for *Endeavour* to head for the safety of the shore. Here the ship was run aground close to the mouth of the river which today bears its name.

Repairs took nearly two months: and in this time Cook was able to carry out a fair amount of exploration, and to make contact with the Aborigines. He formed a favourable impression of both the country and the people. *"The land,"* he wrote, *"is well diversified with Hills and Plains. The soil of the Hills is dry and stoney, yet it produceth a thin grass and a little wood. The soil of the Plains is sandy and friable, and produceth long grasses and Shrubs etc. It is indifferently well watered with many small Brooks but no great Rivers. The Climate is warm and fine, and the air wholsom."* His description of the Aborigines is equally discerning: *"They are an inoffensive race, in no way inclined to cruelty. They have no fix'd habitation, but move from place to place. They may appear to some to be wretched; but in reality are happier than we Europeans. They live in Tranquillity. The Earth and the Sea furnish them with all things necessary."*

When Cook returned to England his report on Australia and its inhabitants aroused great interest. Coffee-house poets extolled the Simple Life of the Noble Savages:
"Can Europe boast, with all her pilfered wealth,
A larger share of happiness or health?"
No wonder that with such an idyllic shore to settle on, the British government decided to press ahead with its plans to establish bases.

2 Convicts and Whalers

Everyone aboard the *Endeavour* had been favourably impressed with Australia, none more so than Midshipman James Matra. When *Endeavour* returned to England, Matra urged the British government to send settlers to *"this new land which should prove most convenient for crops and livestock."* In particular Matra urged that farmers in America who had lost their land as a result of the American War of Independence (1775–1781) should be resettled in Australia. This was a better idea in theory than in practice; for few American farmers were willing to make so long and difficult a journey, not knowing what they were going to find at the end of it. Matra therefore put forward an alternative scheme: that Australia should be settled by convicts, shipped out under a military escort. This, he argued, would 'kill two birds with one stone'. It would relieve overcrowding in British prisons; and it would prevent other nations, in particular the French, from settling in and laying claim to the new-found territory.

The British government liked this idea and gave it their blessing. In March, 1787 the first convict fleet bound for Australia set sail from Spithead in the English Channel.

It was a large fleet: two warships, three supply ships and six transports. Its crew and military escort numbered 233, and there were 759 convicts. Its commander was Captain Arthur Phillip, who was to prove an able and humane leader. Indeed it was due largely to Phillip that the long and difficult voyage to Australia was accomplished without incident and with relatively few casualties. For what a voyage it must have been! The ships were old; the stores were inadequate; the distance covered was enormous (over 24,240 kilometres), and the time taken was equally enormous (over eight months). On such a

Above: Captain Arthur Phillip; and left, the Alexander, one of the six convict transports which made up his fleet.

voyage a death-rate of 20% might have been anticipated – when Anson had sailed round the world in 1741 more than 60% of *his* ship's company had died of scurvy. Yet in the first fleet there was a death-rate of less than 2%. This was partly because Phillip insisted that the convicts were given plenty of fresh food – he stopped three times to reprovision; at Teneriffe, Rio de Janeiro and Cape Town. He made sure they had plenty of fresh air, and were allowed on deck at least once a day for exercise. Also he maintained firm but fair discipline – a marine found guilty of having intercourse with one of the female convicts was given 100 lashes. There were therefore few incidents during the voyage: simply day after day, week after week, month after month of *"sailing over a vast and imperfectly explor'd sea, with not so much as a fish or a bird for company."* Not until they neared the Great Australian Bight was the monotony broken by

their sighting *"great numbers of black whales which kept pace with our ship for many hours."*

This was a prophetic meeting. For it was the convicts and the whales who were, between them, responsible for the founding of Australia.

After a voyage of 24,242 kilometres and 247 days, the fleet dropped anchor in Botany Bay, the site of Cook's original landing in 1770. As he stepped ashore, Phillip must have hoped his troubles were over. In fact they were about to begin.

Botany Bay was not a good place for a settlement. The harbour was shallow and exposed to the easterly winds. The ground was swampy and, in the words of the fleet's doctor, "likely to prove none too healthy". Phillip therefore decided to examine the harbour mentioned by Cook which lay some twenty kilometres to the north. It was a fortunate decision. For the harbour was Sydney. *"I have the honour to inform your Lordship,"* Phillip wrote in his despatches to England, *"that we have had the satisfaction of finding what is surely the finest harbour in the world, in which a thousand (ships) of the line might ride in perfect safety ... It has springs of sweet Water, and numerous sheltered Coves, formed by narrow necks of land covered in Timber."* In one of these coves Phillip and his men were met by a group of Aborigines, who *"waded into the water unarmed and examined our Boat with much curiosity. Their confidence and manly behaviour made me give to this place the name of Manly Cove."* (How many of those who today sunbathe and surf on one of Sydney's best-loved beaches realise it is named after a group of 18th century Aborigines?) The fleet moved to Sydney early in 1788, and on January 26th Phillip took formal possession of the new-found territory. This date is now celebrated as Australia Day. The painting on page 20 gives a romanticised impression of the ceremony.

Although Sydney was an excellent site, the settlement didn't take root easily. Indeed for several years it was touch and go whether the thousand-odd people who landed from the first fleet would survive or die of starvation and disease. For they were afflicted by almost as many trials and tribulations as the Biblical Job. The truth is that Cook had seen Australia

The Founding of Australia. An artist's impression of Captain Arthur Phillip raising the flag at Sydney Cove on 26th January 1788.

through rose-coloured spectacles. The new-found continent was *not* a land flowing with milk and honey. It was a beautiful but harsh land, where the soil is predominantly poor and the climate fluctuates between extremes of heat and cold and drought and flood. It took the settlers some time to adjust to these conditions. To start with their sheep and cattle died. Their seeds were eaten by mice and ants. Their few crops which did struggle through were destroyed by insects or by fungi and bacteria, to which they had no immunity. And what happened to the crops happened also to the people. No sooner had they landed than they were taken ill. Within a week of landing "sickness and scurvy were raging in a manner most extraordinary." We can tell how serious this sickness was by the fact that the first building to be erected at Sydney Cove was a hospital. To add to Phillip's problems, the convicts included a hard core of discontented men, who responded neither to discipline nor kindness.

There was much drunkenness and stealing. It is a wonder that the settlement survived.

But survive it did. Its survival was due to several factors. The British government was unwilling to see it go under, and therefore kept sending in more ships with more convicts and more supplies. A handful of dedicated men on the spot (like the doctor Wentworth and the convict Greenway who designed some of the finest buildings in Sydney) worked tirelessly for the common good. And the convicts and free-settlers managed eventually to build up a small but self-sufficent agricultural community. All this ensured survival. But it was something else that ensured success. Towards the end of the century it was suddenly realised that the settlement had on its doorstep a commodity for which the world was clamouring.

It was not the somewhat arid pastures of New South Wales which brought prosperity to the newborn settlement. It was the richer pastures of the sea.

*   *   *

People have hunted whales for many thousand

years. Originally they hunted them for food and for their fatty blubber which, when lit, was a source of both warmth and light. Then in the 18th century two further uses were found for the unfortunate creatures: their oil was used as a lubricant for the machines of the industrial revolution, and their bones were used for corsets and stays to pull in the waists and elevate the bosoms of fashionable ladies. The resulting increase in the demand for whale-products led to overfishing, and it wasn't long before many species in the northern hemisphere were virtually exterminated. Whalers then turned their attention to the southern hemisphere. Here, however, there were problems. For most of the whales in the south were larger, faster and more difficult to catch than the whales of the north. Also there were no ports close to the whaling grounds where the carcasses could be processed: i.e. reduced to blubber, oil and bone.

Those who sailed in the first convict fleet had sighted whales on both their outward and homeward journeys; and as further reports of sightings continued to come in, it was soon realised that each year one particular type of

Whalers about to harpoon a whale off the coast of Australia.

whale flocked in great numbers to the shores of south-east Australia. These were *Eubalaena australis*, the Southern Right Whales. *Eubalaena australis* were black, peaceful, slow-moving creatures; they spent much of their life in inshore waters, and when they were killed they floated. They therefore became known as the easy whales or the "Right" whales to kill. They were the perfect prey for the whalers. And Sydney – and later Melbourne, Adelaide and Hobart – were perfect ports for the whalers to operate from. Within ten years of Phillip's landing in Botany Bay, British and American whalers were bringing both the brutalities and the profits of their calling to the new settlement.

And what a brutal calling it was . . .

The *Sarah and Elizabeth* hove-to about a kilometre from its quarry, a solitary bull whale asleep on the sunlit waters of the Great Australian Bight. The ship's boats – seaworthy six-metre rowing boats – were lowered. Moving cautiously through the swell, the boats ap-

21

proached their quarry. In the leading boat the harpooner rose to his feet. In his hand was a one-and-a-half metre wooden spear, with a heavy steel head to which was shackled a line and cable, coiled down in the bottom of the boat. When he was a little less than four metres from the whale, the harpooner flung his harpoon with all his strength into the great creature's body. The *Sarah and Elizabeth*'s doctor, Thomas Beale, takes up the story. *"Now the sea becomes lashed into foam by the wounded whale. His head rises into the air, his tail strikes in all directions and his huge body writhes in violent contortions. Suddenly he sounds (dives). The rope runs out through its groove in the boat's bow with lightning vel-*

Whaling was a cruel, dangerous occupation; yet it was of great importance to the early Australian economy.

ocity. It smokes. So great is the heat produced by friction that it bursts into flame. But the alert headsman pours water on it. Soon the boat's 200 fathom (365 metres) of rope are exhausted; but up comes another boat, just in time, and attaches a second rope. And still the sea monster descends. At last, at 600 fathom (1100 metres) he is held . . . But soon he has to return to the surface to breathe; and here his pursuers are waiting. More harpoons and lances are driven into his body. Mad with agony, the whale rolls over and over, coiling the lines about him, jerking the boats half out of the sea. One is upset, and its crew are swimming for their lives . . . Exhausted, the whale's rush subsides, and the fatal lance is driven home. Blood gushing from the terrified creature's nostrils is flung high into the air and all over the men in the boats. His death pangs seize him. His convulsions throw him this way and that. The sea is beaten into a circle of foam, until at last the great creature rolls on to its side and floats, an inanimate mass, on the surface of the sea."

1840's and 1980's
Few cities have developed more rapidly than Australia's state capitals.
Hobart in the late 1840's; below: Hobart today.
Right: Melbourne in about 1840; below right: Melbourne today.

No-one will ever know how many times this terrible scene was acted out during the early years of the 19th century: maybe half-a-million, maybe a million. But the sad fact is that by 1850 so many of the gentle *Eubalaena australis* had been stabbed to death that the species was very nearly extinct.

The whales died, but the settlements lived: nurtured, it would be no exaggeration to say, on the unfortunate animals' blood. For the profits that stemmed from whaling were enormous, and British and American whalers were soon flocking in great numbers to the shores of southeast Australia. They came not only to the major ports, but to dozens of little whaling stations which sprang up in sheltered bays all along the coasts of New South Wales, Victoria, South Australia and Tasmania.

It would be hard to over-emphasise the boost which whaling gave to the settlement and exploration of Australia. For the whalers changed the whole image of the continent. From being on the rim of the known world, Australia suddenly became the centre of a highly profitable international industry. Soon, as the statistics below tell us, the number of whalers in the settlements was far greater than the number of convicts:

Date	Naval and military personnel	Convicts	Free settlers	Whalers
1780	233	759	–	–
1800	625	1,977	311	3,584

Herman Melville, author of the classic sea story *Moby Dick*, hit the nail on the head when he wrote: *"the whaleship is the true mother of that mighty* (Australian) *colony."*

Hindley Street, Adelaide, painted in the 1840's by George Angas.

3 "One land, to which I give the name Australia"

It was May 14th 1801, and *HMS Investigator* was about to sail from the River Thames to try something that had never been tried before: to survey the whole coastline of the lands then known as New Holland and New South Wales. The ship's captain, Matthew Flinders, was organising the loading of their provisions. Already aboard was Flinders' young wife, Annette. They had been married only a few weeks earlier, and Flinders was planning to take Annette with him as far as Sydney. (It was

A contemporary portrait of Captain Matthew Flinders, the first man to circumnavigate Australia and (below) the Flinders Ranges in South Australia, first sighted by his expedition in 1802.

fairly usual in those days for a commander's wife to accompany her husband to sea – one commander actually had his wife aboard during the battle of Trafalgar!) However, as ill luck would have it, one of the Lords of the Admiralty paid an unexpected visit to the *Investigator*, where, we are told, he found Annette Flinders "seated in the captain's cabin, *not wearing a bonnet* (hat)." This lack of a bonnet may not seem to us a very serious

Australia has many unique animals and plants. Above: Platypus, a painting by Ferdinand Bauer who accompanied Flinders on his circumnavigation. Right: Bottlebrush.

matter. However, to the Sea Lord it was a very serious matter indeed. For he considered it *"a clear indication that Mrs. Flinders regarded the ship too much as her home."* The incident was reported to the Admiralty; and the Admiralty told Flinders that he must either leave his wife behind in England or give up command of his ship.

Matthew and Annette were very much in love. But deeply as Flinders cared for his wife, he cared even more for what he thought was his duty and his honour. As a young naval officer he had already charted much of the east coast of Australia. Together with George Bass he had been the first man to sail all the way round Tasmania, and so prove it wasn't part of the mainland; and he had publicly declared it his intention *"to explore these (Australian) coasts so thoroughly that no man after me shall find it necessary to explore again."* So he now wrote: *"Whatever my disappointment, I will give up the wife for the voyage of discovery."*

A few weeks later *Investigator* was southward bound. As Flinders watched the coast of England disappear into the haze, he must have had mixed feelings: pride that at the age of only 28 he was in command of a major voyage of discovery, sadness at having to leave his wife behind. It was as well he didn't know that he and Annette were not to see one another for ten long years, and that when he did at last return to her he would be a dying man.

Flinders tells us that his voyage to Australia was "uneventful". However, *any* long voyage in those days was a challenge; and this was par-

ticularly so aboard the *Investigator*, which was – all too literally – a rotten old ship. The *Investigator* had been long past its prime when the Navy bought it in 1798, and cut gun-ports into its sides to fit it out for convoy duty in the Channel. These gun-ports weakened its hull. But more serious by far was the fact that beneath its smart new copper-sheathing many of the *Investigator's* timbers were rotten. It leaked like the proverbial sieve. *"Wednes 2 Sept 1801,"* Flinders wrote in his Diary, *"the leakiness of the ship increases, and amounts to 5 inches (12 centimetres) of water an hour."* Flinders had the seams recaulked. But if his ship was in such a sorry state at the start of the voyage, what, he must have wondered, would it be like at the end?

Another challenge facing Flinders was the health of his crew. At the beginning of the 19th century conditions aboard the Navy's ships were often appalling: cramped quarters, poor ventilation, stinking bilge-water and non-existent sanitary arrangements. Ill health was normal. Death was frequent. Flinders was much more concerned about the health of his crew than the average ship's captain. However, in matters of hygiene he was not so much an innovator as an imitator. Again to quote his Diary: *"I put into execution the beneficial plan first practiced by the great captain Cook. On every fine day the deck below was cleared, washed, aired with stoves and sprinkled with vinegar. Beds and sea-chests were opened up and expos'd to sun and air. Officers and men were allowed to drink freely from the pump, and there was no restriction to the allowance of fresh water. Lime-juice and sugar acted as antiscorbutics, preventing scurvy. As a result of these regulations my entire crew remained in a state of excellent health."*

But perhaps the greatest challenge for Flinders was his ship's navigation. For when it came to navigating, charting and surveying, Flinders was a perfectionist. He was experimenting with new ideas before the *Investigator* was clear of the English Channel. He was, for example, the first person to understand and try to correct the deviation of a ship's compass. This, he realised, was due to the needle of the compass being attracted by the various pieces of iron which were strengthening the ship. He corrected this by placing "iron stanchions" close to the compass, so that the ship's field of magnetism was evened out. These stanchions, known as Flinders Bars, are still used in ship's compasses today, and add greatly to the accuracy of navigation by sea.

Early in December, 1801 *Investigator* sighted the southwest tip of Australia, and a couple of days later entered the sheltered and beautiful anchorage of King George's Sound. Ahead lay several thousand kilometres of shore which was not only unknown but which few men had set foot on since the beginning of time.

Flinders' survey of Australia was more painstaking than exciting. There was – at least to start with – no shipwreck, no violent storm, no battle with the Aborigines. He discovered no great rivers, no sensational geographical features such as a channel dividing New Holland from New South Wales. Indeed he made no sensational discoveries at all. What he *did* make was an extremely accurate survey of almost every foot of the coast: a survey which not only proved that New Holland and New South Wales were on continuous land, but which established the shape and position of this land with pinpoint accuracy. Flinders' charts were so good that they were still being used in Australia *after* World War II! And as

well as *charting* much of Australia's coast, Flinders also *studied* it. For in addition to his normal crew, he had aboard the *Investigator* a team of highly gifted scientists. There was Robert Brown, one of the greatest naturalists of the century, and a founder-member of the Royal Geographical Society; John Allen, a competent geologist; Peter Good, a competent horticulturalist; and two specialist artists, one of whom, Ferdinand Bauer, was one of the greatest botanical painters of all time. Flinders' sailing orders required him to allow *"these botanical gentlemen every opportunity to range about and collect the produce of the earth and to complete their paintings."* This was something new. In the past, most commanders had regarded scientists and artists as so much unwanted ballast, and had kept them on a tight rein. Flinders was one of the first commanders to take an interest in the work of his scientists and to help them. The result was that the knowledge which stemmed from the voyage of the *Investigator* was probably greater, in scientific terms, than the knowledge which had stemmed from any previous voyage. On the south coast of Australia alone, between January and May 1802 Brown collected and classified no fewer than 750 unknown plants, while Bauer made more than 450 sketches of unknown plants and living creatures. This represented a major addition to botanical and zoological knowledge. Indeed Flinders' voyage round Australia might be regarded as the first of the great truly scientific voyages: a forerunner of Darwin's voyage in the *Beagle* and Nares' in the *Challenger.*

Flinders' Diary describes both the monotony of his work and the bleakness of the shore which unfolded kilometre after thousand kilometre ahead of him.

"January, 1802" (Heading east from King George's Sound.) *"In running along the South Coast I endeavoured to keep as close-in with the land (as I could, so that waves breaking along the shore were ever visible from the deck. In this way no river or opening could escape being seen. Such a close proximity involved much danger and loss of time, and I was constantly at the masthead. All bearings were laid down as soon as taken; and when we haul'd off from the coast at night, every precaution was taken to come in at exactly the same place next morning ..."* *"February, 1802"* (Off the Nullarbor Plain, which is one of the driest coasts on Earth.) *"The prospect of the interior is desolate in the extreme. Sand and stone everywhere presented themselves on the lower levels, and the shining sides of the hills showed them to be still more bare. The vegetation consisted of sparse shrubs which yielded a delightful harvest to the botanists. But to the herdsman and cultivator it promised nothing: not a blade of grass nor a square yard (metre) of soil from which seed could be expected back ..."* *"March, 1802"* (In Spencer Gulf.) *"Messrs. Brown, Bauer and Westall set*

Another of Australia's unique animals, the Kangaroo: painted by a member of Dumont D'Urville's expedition in the late 1830's.

off to ascend the mountains, while I went in a cutter to explore the head of the gulph. Mr. Brown and party had a difficult ascent, but by perseverance gained the top of the highest mountain, where they spent the night. From the summit neither river nor lake could be seen. Looking inland the eye traversed nothing but a flat and waterless plain." It would be hard to imagine a more desolate scene. Yet it was here, on the edge of the outback, that the artist Ferdinand Bauer discovered some of Australia's most beautiful grasses and flowers: grasses and flowers which he painted with unsurpassed accuracy and artistry.

A couple of months later *Investigator* dropped anchor in Sydney Cove. In ten months Flinders had crossed 19,000 kilometres of ocean and charted more than 3,000 kilometres of unknown coast. We can judge how well he must have looked after his crew by the fact that as *Investigator* entered harbour *"every member of the ship's company was on deck in better health and not in less good spirits than on the day we had sailed from Spithead (England)."*

After a short rest in Sydney, *Investigator* continued to head anti-clockwise round Australia. On this second part of the voyage Flinders was no longer breaking new ground, for most of the east and north coasts had already been roughly charted. But once again,

by "keeping all the time within sight of the breaking waves", Flinders carried out a survey of the greatest accuracy and detail. Whereas those who had gone before had produced only a rough sketch, he produced a finished picture. He also continued to make a scientific study of the plants, animals and natural phenomena that he came across. He was, for example, the first person to give a reasoned explanation of how the coral islands of the Great Barrier Reef are formed. *"It seems to me that when the creatures which form the corals at the bottom of the ocean cease to live, their structures adhere to each other, and a mass of rock is formed. Future creatures erect their habitations upon this rock, then die in turn to elevate this monument of their labours. It seems essential to the existence of the creatures that they are constantly covered with water; and at last a solid mass is formed as high as the tides reach. This mass is then visited by sea-birds; salt water plants take root in it, and soil begins to be formed; a cocoa-nut or the seed of a pandanus is thrown on-shore; land birds visit it and drop the seeds of shrubs and trees; at every high tide and every gale something is added to the bank; an island is gradually formed, and last of all comes man to take possession."*

Koalas, amongst the most attractive of Australia's mammals.

This sort of detailed analysis marks the dawn of a new approach to exploration. It was not enough for Flinders and his scientists to discover that the coral reefs were there. They wanted to know *why* they were there, how they were formed, and what role they played in the story of our planet. For almost the first time, the geography of the world was being studied scientifically.

So far things had gone well for Flinders. But this was now to change. His first problem was his crew. They had now been at sea for over a year, and their resistance to fever, dysentery and scurvy had been lowered. In the heat and humidity of the Torres Strait (only 10° south of the equator) their health began to deteriorate. His second problem was his ship. The *Investigator* had leaked ever since leaving England, and it was now taking in so much water that the pumps could scarcely keep pace with the inflow. It may seem surprising that the Admiralty should have sent so wretched a ship on so

important a mission; but because of the long-drawn wars with France all the best warships had to be kept at home. The *Investigator* was all that could be spared. And now, as the ship entered the Gulf of Carpentaria, the leaks became worse. Much worse. Soon water was flooding into the hold at the rate of 35 centimetres an hour. Flinders struggled south to the foot of the Gulf; then did the only possible thing. He ran the *Investigator* aground to allow the ship to be tipped on its side and cleaned, and its seams resealed.

However, as the carpenters set about their work, the reports which they passed back to Flinders became more and more alarming. *"Out of the ten top timbers, one (is) partly rotten and five entirely rotten ... On the larboard (port) quarter the timber is entirely rotten ... On the starboard bow we have seen three timbers which are all rotten ... The stemson is mostly decay'd ... The tree nails are in general rotten (and) with much sea running* the ship would hardly escape foundering." The chief carpenter, Russel Mart, ended his report with the gloomy forecast. "In 12 months there will scarce be a sound timber in her; yet if she remain in fine weather and (there) happen no accident she may run 6 months longer."

This was a bombshell. "I cannot express the surprise and sorrow the carpenters' report gave me," Flinders wrote in his Diary. It seemed that his dream of circumnavigating Australia wouldn't, after all, be realised.

It was obvious that the sooner Investigator got back to Sydney the better. But how? It was now the season when the south-east trade winds were blowing strongly over the Gulf of Carpentaria; and for a leaking sailing-ship to beat back against these winds would have been a daunting, if not impossible, task. The alternative was to continue anti-clockwise all the way round the continent: a far longer voyage, but one for which the winds would be mostly favourable. Flinders decided to go the long way round. From this moment his voyage turned into a race with death. Could he limp back to Sydney before his ship foundered, or his crew succumbed to the dysentery and

scurvy which were now taking an ever-mounting toll? As he ran for safety Flinders had no alternative but to abandon his survey. His object now was not surveying, but surviving.

It took him almost exactly six months to struggle back: a terrible voyage, with his ship near-sinking, and his crew sick, weak and many of them dying. But at last, on 9th June 1803, Investigator limped into Sydney Cove. Flinders was only just in time. For the carpenters who examined his ship found it "totally decayed, and not worth repairing." Many of its timbers were so rotten that a piece of bamboo could be pushed clean through them.

Flinders' achievements had been great. But he himself felt that his job was only half done; for part of the north coast and most of the west coast had not been surveyed in detail. He therefore applied for "another ship with which to examine these uncharted parts." No ship was available in Australia. Flinders therefore set sail for England in the Porpoise, taking with

Below: loss of Porpoise and Cato.

Right: the survivors encamped on a sandbar, from Flinders' A Voyage to Terra Australis.

him many of his crew, his charts and diaries, and Brown's invaluable collection of plants. He must have thought that danger and privation lay behind him, and that ahead lay recognition for his work and a longed-for reunion with the young wife whom he hadn't seen for more than three years.

It was not to be. The rest of Flinders' life was anti-climax. And tragedy.

The *Porpoise*, together with two other ships, the *Bridgewater* and the *Cato*, set sail for England on 10th August 1803. Flinders was not in command, but sailed as a passenger aboard the *Porpoise*. On August 17th, *Porpoise* and *Cato* ran aground on the Great Barrier Reef, and *Bridgewater* most ungallantly sailed off and left them to their fate! Both ships were soon battered to destruction. Their crews, however, managed to struggle to the comparative safety of a nearby sandbar, where they set up a temporary camp. Flinders then took one of *Porpoise*'s boats, and went back to Sydney for help. Eventually everyone was rescued; but Flinders' charts and diaries were badly damaged, while Brown's magnificent collection of plants was almost totally destroyed by salt water. This was a disaster. But worse was to follow.

When Flinders set out a second time for England the only ship available was the *Cumberland*. The *Cumberland* was unbelievably small; the *Investigator* had weighed 334 tonnes, the *Cumberland* weighed 29! The tiny ship, battered by storms and short of food, was forced to take shelter in Mauritius. Mauritius was French, and France and England were at war. Flinders was taken prisoner. He was in fact carrying with him a letter of protection from the French government to say that he was engaged on *bona fide* exploration. This, however, was not honoured, and Flinders was held prisoner for seven long years. His health,

already weakened by his privations aboard the *Investigator*, got steadily worse. Soon he became very ill indeed.

In 1810, as a result of a British naval blockade on Mauritius, Flinders was released. By the end of the year he was back in England, and reunited at last with Annette. There are only two references in contemporary documents to their reunion. But they say it all. First, a note sent to Annette by Flinders' personal servant, warning her of her husband's ill health: *"the Captain does not look so well as he did by a very great deal, his red cheeks is gone and his hair very white."* The other is a note written by a relative, who found Matthew and Annette's reunion *"so affecting that (he) could not bear to remain in the room; nor could (he) be persuaded to call back again that same day."*

Flinders had returned to England at what, for him, was an unfortunate time: when people were more interested in the war with France than in the exploration of a little-known continent at the opposite side of the world. He was retired on half-pay and given little help with preparing his diaries and charts for publication. Desperately ill and desperately short of money, he devoted the last years of his life to writing his monumental work *A Voyage to Terra Australis*, which shares with d'Urville's *Voyage au Pôle Sud* the distinction of being one of the best and most beautiful books on exploration ever written. It was 1814 before *A Voyage to Terra Australis* was published, and by this time Flinders – though only 40 years old – was dying. On 18th July a copy of his book was placed in his hands. But he never saw it. He was in a coma, and died, without regaining consciousness, the next day.

Flinders was a great but unlucky explorer. He gave the world a great deal more than the world gave him.

4 Across the Continent

In the years immediately after Flinders' voyage, settlements sprang up at many places round the coast of Australia. The Great Dividing Range, which runs parallel to the east coast, was crossed, and settlements began to take root along the banks of the Murray, Darling and Lachlan Rivers. Yet all these settlements together added up to less than 5% of the continent. The other 95%, the interior, remained "a blank on the map, a ghastly void".

This was the outback.

The outback is one of the great wilderness-areas of the Earth. It is very dry; in most places there is under 250mm of rain a year. It is very hot; in most places the mid-day temperature *averages* nearly 38°C. It has few oases. It is crossed by no trade routes. Apart from the Sahara, it is the largest area of desert and semi-desert in the world. To give you an idea of its size, one single outback cattle-station (ranch) in the Northern Territory covers a greater area than the whole of England and Wales. Why you might ask, should anyone want to explore such a forbidding wilderness?

Australians began to explore the outback partly because it was a challenge: a frontier on their doorstep ever-waiting to be pushed back, a mystery ever-waiting to be solved. *"Let any man,"* wrote the great explorer Charles Sturt, *"lay the map of Australia before him and regard the blank upon its surface; and then let me ask him if it would not be an honourable achievement to be the first to place foot in its centre."* But there was another and more practical reason for exploration. By the middle of the 19th century the Australian whaling and sealing industries had collapsed, since the unfortunate animals had been virtually exterminated. Gold had not yet been discovered. The settlements had therefore to rely on farming to survive. This was the age of wool,

and to a lesser degree the age of beef. In the decade 1840–1850 the number of sheep and cattle in Australia almost doubled. Finding new pastures for these ever-increasing flocks and herds became an economic necessity; and it was in search of such pastures that explorers began to push into the outback. This accounts for the fact that many of those who explored Australia were local men: practical surveyors (like Forrest and the Gregory brothers) or practical farmers (like Eyre and Sturt). Other continents were nearly always explored by outsiders – Livingstone for example in Africa, Amundsen in Antarctica, Elias in Asia. Australia was explored by Australians.

This was as well, For those who lived in the shadow of the outback and understood it, were most likely to survive its rigours. It is no co-incidence that it was the outsiders who were involved in most of the tragedies of Australian exploration: men from Germany like Leichhardt, and men from Great Britain like Burke and Wills.

The story of one of these tragedies, that of Burke and Wills, shows all too clearly what was likely to happen to those who ventured into the outback without understanding it, and with more courage than discretion.

Robert O"Hara Burke was born in 1821 in Galway (Ireland). He was an adventurer, who had served in the Belgian infantry, the Hungarian cavalry and the Melbourne police. William John Wills was born in 1834 in Devon (England). He was a doctor, with a keen interest in meteorology and surveying. The two men were as different as chalk from cheese. Burke was flamboyant and extrovert, Wills was quiet and self-effacing. In 1859 Burke was chosen to lead the Victorian Exploring Expedition, which was planning to attempt the first-ever crossing of the continent. Unfortunately, at much the same time, a South Australian Exploring Expedition, led by Stuart, was about to attempt the same feat. Human nature being what it is, the crossing turned into a race. And in this (as in Scott's and Amundsen's race to the South Pole) lay the seeds of tragedy.

The Victorian Exploring Expedition set out from Melbourne on August 20th, 1860. It was a large and well-equipped expedition, with

Left: Robert O'Hara Burke. Right: William John Wills. The first men to cross Australia from south to north.

twenty-seven camels, twenty-three horses and fifteen men. It took their advance-guard less than three months to reach Cooper's Creek, a little to the east of Lake Eyre. Here a supply depot was established, close to a permanent waterhole, and the expedition split up. William Brahe stayed behind with orders to establish a camp; while Burke, Wills, King and Gray made a dash for the north coast. The north-coast team took with them six camels and a horse, and supplies for four months – though Burke optimistically reckoned they could complete the 2,400 kilometre journey in three months.

Too much has been written about Burke's failure: too little about his success. For his success in reaching the north coast and so being the first person ever to cross the Australian continent, was a magnificent achievement.

Burke and his companions set out on 16th December, and soon settled into an economic routine. Burke and Wills walked ahead, keep-ing their direction by compass. Next came Gray leading the horse. Last came King leading the camels. All seven animals were laden with food and water. The going was never easy; and soon they came to the desert which a few years earlier had halted the explorer Charles Sturt. Sturt's description of this desert has never been bettered. *"The ground over which we advance is covered with pebbles of quartz, ironstone, whinstone and granite – as if McAdam had thrown down every cartload of stones he had ever collected. The thermometer stands at 108° (42°C) in the shade; the heat is intolerable. The men complain of disordered bowels and sore eyes . . . We climbed a small sandhill. From the top the view was sufficient to depress the spirits of anyone. The horizon was level as that of the sea; a deathlike hue pervaded the scene; no living creature save ants were to be seen – even the flies were absent. This desert is silent as the grave, and surely the most gloomy that ever man has trod."* To the north of Sturt's Stony Desert, Burke and Wills came to the Diamantina, one of those billabongs (or seasonal creeks) which, after the rains, run from nowhere to nowhere.

Left: A confident start to Burke and Wills' expedition from the Royal Park, Melbourne, as seen by a contemporary artist.

Above: Crossing the Terrick-Terrick Plains, Victoria; a painting by the expedition's artist, Ludwig Becker.

"Here," wrote Burke, "we found a great many natives who presented us with fish, and offered us their women... Loaded camels and horse with 900 pints (510 litres) of water." Water to start with was their chief anxiety. Yet as they plodded north, the plains became less barren and the billabongs more frequent. Wills, indeed, describes the country as "rough, but with an abundance of fuel and water." In a month they covered 800 kilometres. Things were going well.

Their troubles started when they came to the tropics. The Australian tropics are hot, humid and unhealthy. Burke's expedition arrived at a bad time: in the wet season. Day after day the tepid rain poured down on them. Their camels floundered about in the boggy ground, groaning and moaning. Their horse, Billy, became so weak he could hardly walk. It took them a month to cover the final 300 kilometres to the coast: a nightmare journey, squelching through soft clay and often up to their knees in water. And at the end of it all they never actually saw the sea; for they were brought up short by impenetrable mangrove swamps at the mouth of the Flinders River. "It would have been well," Burke wrote wistfully, "to say that we reached the sea, but we could not obtain a view of the open ocean, although we made every endeavour to do so." They were, however, in salt and tidal water, no more than a couple of kilometres from the Gulf of Carpentaria; and it would be churlish to deny that they were indeed the first people ever to cross the continent from south to north.

On February 13th, 1861 they began the long trek back to their depot on Cooper's Creek.

We don't know a great deal about their journey back. Burke kept no diary. Wills no longer kept a detailed record; the entries in his notebook become progressively shorter and his writing progressively shakier. Reading between the lines, however, it is clear that the four men grew steadily weaker. This was

37

probably because they didn't have enough to eat, and in particular not enough Vitamin C. We know that Burke fixed their daily ration at *"12 small strips of dried meat and ¼ lb (112 grams) flour per man"*; and this, in view of their physical exertions, simply wasn't enough. Soon all four of them were suffering from dysentery, debilitation, giddiness and scurvy. Gray was the worst. *"Charley again very unwell,"* wrote Wills early in March, *"and unfit to do any-thing."* A month later they woke one morning to find Charley Gray had died in his sleep. It indicates how weak the others were that it took a full day to scoop out a shallow grave for him.

The remaining three struggled on, killing several of their camels and eventually their horse, Billy, for meat; until at last, in mid-April, they were nearing the Cooper River. Their ordeal, it seemed, would soon be over. How they must have longed for the food, rest and companionship which, they had every reason to expect, was waiting for them at their depot. Buoyed up by expectation, they made a supreme effort and covered the final 50 kilometres to the Cooper in a single day.

A little after 7 p.m. on 21st April they were approaching the waterhole where their depot was sited. The scrub was silent and bathed in moonlight. *"I think I can see their tents,"* Burke kept saying. *"I think I see them."*

But he was wrong.

The depot, when they did at last stumble into it, was deserted. No tents. No animals. No people. Yet the ash in the fireplace was still warm, and the horse and camel droppings had not yet hardened. Cut into the trunk of a tree near the centre of the camp was a message telling them to dig one metre to the northwest. This they did, and found a box in which was the message: *"Depot, Cooper's Creek, 21st April 1861. The depot party of the V.E.E.* (Victorian Exploring Expedition) *leaves this camp today to return to the Darling ... No person has been up here from the Darling. We have six camels and twelve horses in good working condition. William Brahe."*

They couldn't believe it: that after all they

Despair at Cooper's Creek: a painting by Sir John Longstaff.

had been through they should find themselves deserted. And perhaps the most agonising thing of all about Brahe's message was the date. After walking some 2,500 kilometres in 127 days Burke, Wills and King had missed their companions by only a few hours. The depot party had pulled out that very morning. As the three men looked at one another, they must have had the same fear in their hearts: that the message they'd just read was their death sentence. They sunk to the ground in despair. It was quite a while before they could force themselves to make an inventory of the stores which Brahe had left for them, and a plan.

They found that Brahe had left sufficient food for a month, but nothing else. As for a plan, they decided to rest for a couple of days in the depot, then follow Cooper's Creek towards Mount Hopeless, where they knew there was a police station, and safety. Mount Hopeless was only 240 kilometres away. It didn't *sound* far. But by now the three of them were so weak that King, that evening, had to crawl to the creek to get water on his hands and knees.

On April 23rd they set out for Mount Hopeless. They had two camels and a reasonable supply of food, and there seemed to be plenty of water. However, to quote Alan Moorehead, *"the Cooper is an unpredictable stream. In a year of exceptional rainfall the water comes down with a roar, and for dozens of miles across the flat land there is nothing to be seen but a brown flood with the tops of trees appearing above it. But this only happens every ten years or so. Normally the creek fans out into innumerable channels, which soon dry up into chains of waterholes and billabongs; and the farther you go down the creek towards Lake Eyre (and Mount Hopeless) the drier it becomes, until in the end every channel peters out into rocks and sand. It does not matter which you follow; always you end up among sandhills and waterless plains of sharp red rock. It is not sinister country – it is too bright and open for that – but the spaces are vast, the sun pitiless and the hours pass in a torpor. Torpor, inertia – this is what overcomes the traveller, especially if he is on foot."* And soon Burke and his companions *were* on foot; for

Cooper's Creek as it is today. Above: the tree on which instructions to dig were left for Burke and Wills. Right: the desolate appearance of the creek.

their camels got bogged down in the quicksands round the waterholes and had to be shot. For awhile the three men struggled on, moving slower and slower, growing weaker and weaker. Then, realising they hadn't the strength to reach Mount Hopeless, they gave up and retraced their steps towards their original depot. Here, at least, they knew there was water. Back at their depot, they were looked after by a tribe of nomadic Aborigines, who managed to keep them alive for quite some time with gifts of fish and nardoo seed. *"The blacks,"* wrote Wills in his diary, *"are very hospitable and attentive."* But the Aborigines could only delay the end; they couldn't prevent it. Wills died of starvation and exhaustion on about July 1st and Burke a few days later. The only survivor was King, whom a relief party found three months later *"in an appalling state, burnt black by the sun and half mad with starvation and loneliness."*

It was a tragic end to an expedition that had achieved so much.

There was, of course, a *post mortem*. People wanted to know who to blame. For more than a hundred years the finger has usually been pointed at the unfortunate Burke. The Royal Commission appointed by the Victorian government to look into the disaster wrote: *"Mr. Burke* (showed) *greater zeal than prudence in departing from Cooper's Creek before the main depot party had arrived, and without having secured communications with the settled districts; and in undertaking so extended a journey with insufficient provisions . . . It does not appear that Mr. Burke kept any regular journal. Had he performed this essential portion of the duty of a leader, many of the calamities of the expedition might have been avoided."* This may have a weighty ring to it; but it is nonetheless nonsense. For in pushing on as fast as he could Burke was simple obeying the orders of the Victorian Exploring Committee; and how could it have made the slightest different to the fate of his expedition if he had kept the most detailed of Diaries? It seems to me more likely that the *real* culprits were William Brahe, who withdrew from Cooper's Creek before he need have; and the members of the Victorian Exploring Committee, who first chose Burke as their expedition-leader in spite of his inexperience of the outback, and then told him they wanted him to be the first man to cross the continent, "for the honour of Victoria". *"Stuart,"* wrote the Committee chairman, *"has already left Adelaide, so it will . . . be a race between you and he."* However, perhaps the final word on the tragedy should be left to the man whose ability and conduct were at all times beyond reproach: the gentle and self-effacing Wills. A few days before he died, Wills wrote in a letter to his father: *"Cannot possibly last more than a fortnight. But it is consolation to know that we have done all we could, and that our deaths will be the result of mismanagement of others* (rather) *than any rash act of our own."*

Let that be their epitaph.

5 The Exploration of the Outback

Burke's crossing of the continent was *not* typical of the way the outback was explored. It was, like Scott's dash for the South Pole, an isolated act of competitiveness, the tragic end of which has brought it notoriety. Most explorers of the outback were more knowledgeable than Burke; and within the span of a generation these tough and knowledgeable men had unveiled the secrets of the Australian deserts and filled in the "ghastly blank" on the map. If asked to name the greatest of them, I would choose Sturt, Eyre, Leichhardt, Stuart, Gregory, Warburton and Forrest. The diaries of these brave and dedicated explorers tell us of the hazards they had to face.

Charles Sturt (1795–1869) used to be thought of as "a mere traveller", but it is now generally accepted that he was the father of Australian exploration. Between 1828 and 1830 he explored the Darling and Murray Rivers: journeys which helped to open up new grazing lands to the west of the Great Dividing Range. His finest achievement, however, was his expedition in search of the inland sea, which was believed in those days to lie in the heart of the outback. Sturt left Adelaide in August 1844 with four wagons, eleven horses, fifteen men, sixty bullocks and 300 sheep. He also took with him a boat which, optimistically, he hoped to launch on the inland sea when he had found it.

"October 9th," he wrote in his Diary, *"we have now arrived at the borders of the desert which has so far foiled the most enterprising explorers. The natives are not encouraging. They say 'if you go into the desert your bullocks will hang out their tongues, your waggons will tip over, and you will die. For there is neither water nor grass in the desert, not a stick to light fire with.'"* A couple of months later: *"The ranges have now ceased, and we have all around us a level boundless expanse, without*

The Olgas, Northern Territory, rise from a level plateau.

a landmark to guide us. The temperature stands at 118° (47°C) in the shade. So great is the heat that every screw in our boxes has been drawn (loosened). *The horn handles of our instruments and our combs have split. The lead drops out of our pencils. Our hair has ceased to grow; and our nails have become brittle as glass. Scurvy afflicts us all. We are attacked by violent headaches, pains in the limbs, and swollen and ulcerated gums. Mr. Poole* (the expedition surveyor) *grew worse and worse; the skin over his muscles became black, and he lost the use of his lower extremities. On the 14th* (July) *he expired . . . Nothing could exceed the sterile character of this terrible desert, or the hopelessness of the prospect before us. But the moon being full we continued our journey, at times across the dry white bed of salt lagoons, at other times along the top of sandy ridges. The sky is cloudy, but no rain ever falls. We are struggling against difficulties such as are not to be overcome by human perseverence.*" Sturt forced his way to within 240 kilometres of the centre of the continent. Then, very wisely, he gave up and

returned to Adelaide. This was a great if inconclusive journey, for which the Royal Geographical Society awarded Sturt its gold medal, congratulating him in particular on "the prudence with which farther advance was abandoned." One of the characteristics of good – as distinct from dead – explorers is that they know when to give up.

An explorer who travelled even greater distances than Sturt, across an even more terrible desert, was Eyre.

Edward John Eyre (1815–1901) was an overlander, a man whose experience in driving vast herds of cattle over vast distances made him an expert traveller in the Australian bush. And how important it was that those who ventured into the outback should be practical bushmen. To quote Feeken and Spate's splendid book *The Discovery and Exploration of Australia:* "*Bushcraft was vital. Not just success, but life itself often depended on it . . . Water, water, water – the word runs like a refrain through the* (explorers') *journals. The flight of birds, a line of dark bush, the trend of a dried-up creek bed, even the settling of a*

single bird on a desert plain – such were the clues which meant water, and it took keen eyes to detect them and a bushman's experience to evaluate them." Eyre had to call on all his bushcraft to survive in the Nullarbor Plain. The Nullarbor Plain is a 1,600 kilometre stretch of desert running parallel to the Great Australian Bight. It is one of the most desolate coastal plains on Earth. In February, 1841 Eyre set out from Fowlers Bay, in South Australia, hoping to find a stock-route along which the settlers could drive their cattle across the plains to Albany, in Western Australia. For a great deal of his journey he had only one companion, an Aborigine named Wylie. Within a couple of weeks of setting out Eyre and Wylie were close to dying of thirst. *"March 10th,"* he wrote in his Diary. *"It was clear that unless I discovered water in the morning our horses must perish, whilst it would be doubtful if we ourselves could succeed in saving our*

Left: John Edward Eyre who, with the Aborigine tracker Wylie, explored the waterless Nullarbor Plain (below) in Western Australia.

lives." He saw that someone had been digging in the great white sand-dunes which lined the shore; and in this most unlikely of places he found a lifesaving well. After a brief rest he and Wylie struggled on, pestered by flies and tortured by heat and thirst. In April they survived only by collecting and drinking dew. In May they survived only by sucking the roots of the few straggling eucalypts which grew in the shade of the dunes. In June they were saved only by a chance meeting with the crew of a French whaler. Twice they went for almost a week with neither food nor water. It was July before they struggled through to Albany, having covered 1,800 kilometres of near-waterless desert – mostly on foot – in 132 days. They found no stock-route. They had, however, accomplished an epic journey for which Eyre, like Sturt, was awarded the gold medal of the Royal Geographical Society. One can't help wishing that Wylie too had been given a medal.

The next great explorer to challenge the outback paid the penalty for *not* being an expert bushman.

Friedrich Leichhardt (1813–*circa* 1849) was born in Germany and spent much of his childhood in England.. He arrived in Sydney in 1841, and quickly made a name for himself as a botanist. He had been in Australia only a couple of years, and was certainly no bushman, when he applied to join an expedition which was hoping to pioneer an overland route between Sydney and Port Essington (not far from present-day Darwin). This expedition, however, was so slow in getting off the ground that Leichhardt lost patience and decided to form an expedition of his own. His friends, fearing for his safety, did their best to discourage him; but businessmen and farmers, anxious to find new grazing lands, provided him with money and equipment. So it was a large and well-equipped expedition which headed north from Sydney in the spring of 1844. Leichhardt's Diary reflects his enthusiasm. *"I can hardly master my feelings as I march behind the long line of my companions and horses . . . for what will people say when I reappear with a heap of* (new) *mountain ranges, rivers and creeks in my pocket!"* When

A portrait of Friedrich Leichhardt.

he came to the Mackenzie his enthusiasm knew no bounds: *"This is fine country, covered with rich grass and well watered. Here are open forests, and plains well stocked with game; the honey is sweet as that of Hymettus, and the air is fragrant with wild thyme and marjoram. No country could be better adapted for pastoral purposes."* This sort of description is repeated again and again as Leichhardt made his way north through Queensland; and when he isn't enthusing over the beauties of the country, he is enthusing over the joys of the camp-fire. *"As night advances, the Black fellows' songs die away. The neighing of the tethered horse, the distant tinkling of the bell, or the occasional cry of night birds is all that interrupts the silence of our camp. The fire gets gradually dull, and smoulders slowly under the large pot in which our meat is simmering, while the bright stars pass unheeded over the heads of the dreaming wanderers."* Leichhardt is one of the few explorers who seems really to have *enjoyed* exploring! He

45

The River Leichhardt in northwest Queensland, explored in 1844.

arrived at Port Essington in triumph after a journey of sixteen months and 2,900 kilometres. This was a fine achievement.

Leichhardt, however, was not content to rest on his laurels; and the congratulations had barely died down when he was setting out again, attempting this time to cross the continent from east to west. He didn't get very far. His livestock strayed. His companions fell victim to scurvy. The rivers he was following dried up. His expedition struggled back in confusion after covering only a few hundred kilometres, thankful to escape with their lives. In spite of this near-disaster, and in spite of the warnings of his friends, Leichhardt was soon off a third time, saying that he *"intended to follow the* (River) *Barcoo north to the Gulf of Carpentaria"*. He was never heard of again. For what he didn't realise, until too late, was that the Barcoo *doesn't* flow into the Gulf of Carpentaria. After some 240 kilometres of flowing north, it swings suddenly west into the

central deserts, to lose itself in the treacherous and ephemeral waterholes around Cooper's Creek. Here, at the end of some unknown chain of billabongs, the country which Leichhardt loved so dearly extracted a terrible price for his enthusiasm.

A man who explored a far more barren part of Australia – and survived – was Stuart.

John McDouall Stuart (1815–1865) spent the greater part of his life exploring and surveying the central deserts. In 1860 he became the first person to reach the geographical centre of the continent. Here he climbed a small hill which, in honour of his friend, he named Central Mount Sturt. Next year, trying to cross the continent from south to north, he got as far as Newcastle Waters. From here he made no fewer than eleven attempts to force his way to the Gulf of Carpentaria. Every attempt was unsuccessful – which enables us to see the achievement of Burke and Wills in its true perspective. In 1862 Stuart set out on yet another expedition, and this time, six months after leaving Adelaide, he managed at last to reach the Gulf of Carpentaria. *"Stopped the horses,"* he wrote, *"whilst I advanced to the beach, and was delighted to behold the waters of the Indian Ocean . . . I dipped my feet and washed my face and hands in the sea, as I promised I would do if I reached it."* His journey back was a nightmare. The horses were weak; food and water were scarce; and Stuart himself fell victim to scurvy and near-blindness. On August 3rd he suffered a stroke, which left him partially paralysed and in constant pain. *"What a miserable life mine is now,"* he wrote. *"I get no rest from this terrible gnawing pain; the nights are too long and the days are too long, and I am so weak I am hardly able to move about the camp."* For awhile he was carried between two horses on a specially-made stretcher. Then, on October 27th, he suffered "another stroke of terrible violence". No-one expected him to survive. *"Have asked King and Nash,"* he wrote, *"to sit with me in case of my dying during the night, for it would be lonely for one man to be there by himself."* But, against all the odds, he did survive; and in 1863 he struggled back to Adelaide. Stuart was a fine explorer and a fine man. Like that other great explorer, Ernest Shackleton, he never lost a man on any of his expeditions. He was popular with his fellow-explorers, and more than generous. He was first to reach the centre of the continent, and first to cross it and survive. The telegraph line from Adelaide and Darwin follows the route that he pioneered: so do the railway and the Stuart Highway. One would have liked to say that his achievements were recognised in his own lifetime and rewarded. But this was not so. Both the British government and the South Australian government refused him a pension. Half-crippled, half-blind and wholly unable to work, his last years would have been spent in squalor and poverty if the Royal Geographical Society hadn't championed his cause and managed to win for him "a compensatory award". Few explorers have given so much, and been given so little so grudgingly in return.

Another explorer who was helped by the Royal Geographical Society, though in a very different way, was Augustus Gregory.

Augustus Charles Gregory (1819–1905) was the oldest of four brothers all of whom helped

Augustus Gregory, leader of the North Australian Expedition.

to explore the outback. In 1855 he led a combined land-and-sea expedition which was backed by the Society, the British government and local farmers. It was a large and well-equipped expedition: two ships, the *Monarch* and the *Tom Tough*, fifty horses, 200 sheep, provisions for a year and a half, and eighteen men including a doctor, a geologist, a botanist and that talented and much-travelled artist Thomas Baines. The moment they arrived at the mouth of the Victoria River, near the border between Western Australia and the Northern Territory, the expedition ran into difficulties. The *Monarch* grounded. It took a fortnight to refloat the ship, and during this fortnight the sheep and horses which were still aboard couldn't be landed; many of them died. A few days later the *Tom Tough* got out of control, was swept downriver from sandbar to sandbar, and shipped so much water that many of the expedition's stores and provisions were ruined. To add to Gregory's problems his men suffered from diarrhoea, vomiting and partial blindness. They were attacked by Aborigines; and they quarrelled among themselves. Eventually Gregory split his unwieldy team into two: a sea-expedition which set out in the *Tom Tough* to chart the coastline, and a land-expedition which first explored the Victoria River, then cut across Arnhem Land and into that part of Northern Queensland which had been visited by Leichhardt. The distances they travelled were enormous. Gregory himself covered at least 8,000 kilometres, most of it on foot. Neither the sea nor the land expedition made any dramatic or unexpected discoveries; but they did, between them, chart more than 1,600 kilometres of little-known coast, and map more than 2,000,000 hectares of little-known land. This was a worthy, if unspectacular achievement.

Gregory had a hard time exploring the coast of North Australia. Warburton had an even harder time exploring the interior.

Peter Egerton Warburton (1813–1887) was the first explorer to cross the Great Sandy and Gibson Deserts. These deserts are the most arid and lifeless in the outback, and to cross them Warburton relied on camels. In 1873 he headed west from Alice Springs, his objectives *"to search for pastoral areas to the west of the telegraph line* (between Adelaide and Darwin), *and if possible penetrate to the north-west coast."* Within a few days of leaving Alice Springs, Warburton *"had to settle down for the night without water"*, an entry in his Diary which was to be repeated often during the next eight months. For time and again, as they headed into the very heart of the outback, his expedition found themselves within a hairsbreadth of dying of thirst. And time and again they were saved at the last moment by finding one of the desert's infrequent waterholes. Twice they were rescued from certain death by following Aborigines to their tribal wells; once it was the flight of a flock of diamond-sparrows that led them to water. They found no

Thomas Baines, who accompanied Gregory's expedition of 1855/6 was a brilliant artist and an explorer in his own right. His painting Waterfall on Jasper Creek *(below) shows the testing conditions the expedition had to face on land. His paintings of the* Messenger *and its longboat (opposite) show the expedition's ships which explored the north coast of Australia.*

The long boat of the Messenger attacked by natives pretending to sell turtle near South Wessell Island Gulf of Carpentaria Aug ... 1866

The Messenger attached to the North Australian Expedition passing Vancouver's Reef near Bald Head at the entrance of King George's Sound Feby or March 1857 the wind which had been fresh suddenly fell light and shifted so as to throw her on to the reef with a heavy swell setting the same way "pastoral areas". The land they passed through consisted of an endless succession of barren ranges, stony deserts, and plains carpeted by the dreaded spinifex or triodia grass. Triodia grass is dreaded because, in the words of the naturalist-and-explorer H.W. Bates who edited Warburton's Diaries, *"it is one of the most cheerless objects an explorer can meet. For the country it loves to dwell in is utterly useless for pastoral purposes."* More than half of their camels died. Warburton himself became so weak that he had to be strapped to his camel's back. *"What is to become of us,"* he wrote, *"I dare not think".* At the end of six months his expedition had struggled two-thirds of the way to the coast. They had now passed the point of no return, and had no option but to press on. Soon they came to an endless succession of sand-dunes, running, like the waves of a petrified sea, across their line of advance. Progress became slower and slower. In a month Warburton advanced no more than 65 kilometres

The search for grazing land motivated many of the expeditions to the Outback. Below: droving in the Northern Territory.

to the west. *"Our condition is so critical,"* he wrote, *"that should it please God to give us once more water, I am determined to risk everything, and make a final push for the River Oakover. Some of us might make it, if not all."* Many times during this last terrible stage of their journey it seemed that only a miracle could save them; but at last they struggled through to the headwaters of the Oakover. To say that they were only just in time would be an understatement. For as they half-fell half-stumbled down to the Oakover, every one of their water-containers had been empty for thirty-six hours, and both men and camels were in the final stages of exhaustion. Another dozen hours, another dozen kilometres and they would almost certainly have perished. *"We were all very thankful,"* wrote the laconic Warburton, *"to have escaped with our lives out of this most horrid desert."*

Other explorers of the outback travelled greater distances than Warburton, none travelled over more difficult terrain – except perhaps Forrest.

John Forrest (1847–1918) was a surveyor, who mapped vast areas of the outback with painstaking accuracy. Of his three great

journeys, the last, in 1874, was the most important. He set out from Shark Bay, on the northwest coast, intending to cut diagonally across the continent to Adelaide, on the southeast coast. The first part of his journey was relatively easy. So was the last part. The long central section, however, lay through some of the most barren areas of the outback: 2,400 arid kilometres across the Gibson and Great Victorian Deserts and the Baker, Cavanagh and Musgrave Ranges. Finding water, in this forbidding wilderness, made the difference not just between success and failure, but between life and death. Forrest was both skilful and lucky. Time and again, like Warburton, just when it seemed he would have to give up, he managed to find a waterhole. Here his party would drink and bottle a few litres of brackish water: enough to enable them to struggle on until, a couple of days later, their water was exhausted, and they faced the same crisis all over again. Without his faithful Aborigine trackers, it is doubtful if Forrest would have

survived. But at last, after a journey of more than six months, he came to the overland telegraph line to the north of Adelaide. *"Long and continued cheers,"* he wrote, *"came from our little band as* (we) *beheld at last the goal to which we had been travelling for so long."*

Forrest's journey marks the end of an era. After his three great expeditions no-one could speak any more of "ghastly blanks" on the map. The outback had been crossed and re-crossed from south to north and west to east. It was no longer *terra incognita*. And these great feats of exploration had all taken place in little more than a single generation. To quote the then President of the Royal Geographical Society: *"In Australia the maps of 1830 show little more than a coastline. Yet now* (in 1880) *the arid wastes of the interior have been traversed . . . and on no fewer than ten occasions the Society has awarded its gold medal to an Australian explorer. For the enormous distances of this waterless land, and the difficulty of transit, give a special grandeur to Australian exploration."*

The *exploration* of the outback is a story of which Australians can be proud.

The *exploitation* of this harshly beautiful

Mining in its infancy. The Kapunda Copper Mine in South Australia painted by Angas in the 1840's.

Mining today: opencast mining in New South Wales.

wilderness is not such a happy story. For little has been done to conserve its resources, and even less to safeguard its indigenous people.

As regards conservation, the farmers by and large have acted responsibly. Today, thanks to artesian wells and irrigation, much land which once was wilderness has been brought to life. The miners, in contrast, have sometimes taken much from the land. No sane person would wish to deny Australians the profits which stem from their Aladdin's cave of minerals. However, the minerals are not inexhaustible. They are, like the Right whales, an asset which one day will vanish if they are not properly conserved.

As for the people of the outback, their story is a sad one. Farmers, pushing into the deserts with their cattle and sheep, needed land and water. So they drove the Aborigines out of their tribal grounds and away from their wells. On more than one occasion wells used by Aborigine families were deliberately poisoned with arsenic. Then came the miners, seeking first gold, then coal, iron, copper, zinc and tin, and more recently uranium. The miners also took away the Aborigines' land. But the fact is that an Aborigine depends on his land as a bird depends on air. To quote Colin Simpson's excellent book *Adam in Ochre: "The Australian Aborigine does not transplant. His altars are waterholes, hills and rocks. He is, by the nature of his beliefs, identified with and bound to a particular patch of earth, his tribal land."* Robbed of the land which meant so much to them, the Aborigines lost the will to live. They died in their hundreds-of-thousands. Many of those who didn't die settled on the outskirts of white communities and took to drink. Fifty years ago there was a very real danger that the race would cease to exist. Today, thanks to a growing awareness of their plight, especially among young people, things are looking a little brighter for the Aborigines. A little, but not much. For many Australians still regard these gentle hunter-gatherers of the desert as children of a lesser god.

6 Saving the Great Barrier Reef

Australia has a wealth of unusual plants, animals and marine life, which exist nowhere else on Earth. For some time Australians showed little interest in conserving this unique heritage. In recent years, however, they have taken unprecedented steps to preserve the most important of their treasures: the Great Barrier Reef.

The Great Barrier Reef is the largest and most magnificent area of corals in the world. Its sheer size is staggering. For it runs parallel to the coast of Australia for 2,000 km, from Torres Strait in the north to the Tropic of Capricorn in the south, and extends on average more than 150km offshore. Its total area is over 340,000 square km, which means it is far bigger than Tasmania and Victoria combined. It consists of roughly 2,500 individual coral-formations, the small ones no more than a few metres in length, the big ones stretching for many kilometres. These coral-formations pulsate with life. They are the home of 240 different species of birds, 300 different species of corals, 1,500 different species of fish, 4,000 different species of molluscs, and no fewer than 10,000 different species of sponges. They are also the home of several of the world's endangered creatures: turtles, for example, and dugongs. But even more impressive than the Reef's size and diversity is its beauty. Those who know it and have seen for themselves its riot of colour and life all describe it as a new and wonderful world. *"Until I dived off the Reef,"* a recent visitor said to me, *"I never realised there was another world beneath the sea."*

There were almost certainly no corals off the coast of Australia until about 25 million years ago. Not until the continent had drifted well away from the Pole and into the tropics could corals begin to form. It seems that as Australia moved nearer to the tropics, part of the con-tinent became depressed, and a shallow marine basin was formed off the north-east coast. In this basin temperature and salinity were ideal for the forming of coral, and reefs began to rise in profusion from the bed of the sea. A coral reef consists of the skeletons of what were once tiny, living, lime-secreting organisms. These organisms flourish in warm, shallow, salty water. When the organisms die, their bodies fall to the bed of the sea, and become compacted one on top of another to form a limestone base. Other corals attach themselves to this base, where they live and eventually die; so that, in time, great walls of coral (some of them hundreds of metres high) are built up from the bed of the sea. This dead inner core of coral is usually covered with a living outer layer of the most beautiful sea-creatures and plants.

Off the north-east coast of Australia this reef-

A diver off the Great Barrier Reef investigating the deadly Crown-of-Thorns.

Varieties of coral from the Great Barrier Reef. Left (above): mushroom coral of the Fungia species; Left (below): frilly coral Turbinaria species ; and above a sea-fan or gorgonian, Melithaeidae species.

building continued intermittently right through until the beginning of the Pleistocene era, some million years ago. Then the Earth grew suddenly colder. Water became locked up in the great Polar ice-caps. The level of the sea fell, probably by as much as 50 metres. As the sea receded, so the coral-structures became exposed. Soon they no longer rose as reefs out of the water, but as cliffs out of the land. Indeed, to the people who first sighted them, some 20,000 years ago, they must have appeared as great limestone escarpments, several kilometres inland.

The first people to set eyes on these escarpments were almost certainly Negrito Aborigines. We know that Aborigines lived here, because archaeologists have found the shells of the sea-food they ate, and the pictures of the turtles and fishes they painted on the walls of their caves. Then the Earth grew warmer

again. The ice-caps melted. The sea rose; and the limestone escarpments were turned once more into reefs. About 5,000 years ago the water stabilised at about its present level, leaving the Reef very much as it is today.

It is difficult to say how important a role the Reef has played in shaping Australian history. But it is possible that, by acting as a barrier, it helped to preserve the continent's isolation from the rest of the world. If you look at a map of the Earth's winds and currents, you will see that both the South East Trade Winds and the South Equatorial Current might have been expected to sweep rafts, canoes and sailing ships west from the Polynesian islands and on to the coast of Australia. This westward movement of people took place everywhere else in the Pacific, from New Zealand to the Philippines. Yet there is no legend of Polynesian raiding-parties ever setting foot on Australian beaches, no hint of Polynesian genes among Australian Aborigines. This, I suggest, is because the Reef acted as a barrier. And in the days of sailing ships what a terrible barrier the reefs must have been!

Above: Many exotic fish live close to the Reef. Long-beaked Coral-fish, Chelmon rostratus.

We don't know for certain who was the first European to sight the Reef. It *could* have been sighted by a Portuguese as early as 1540. It was *definitely* sighted in 1768 by Bougainville. The great French navigator in his ship *Etoile* approached the coast of Australia from the east, and saw what looked like an endless succession of shoals and rocks on which the sea thundered with great violence. Bougainville very prudently altered course. *"In the thunder of surf,"* he wrote *"we heard the voice of God, and obeyed it."* What happened a couple of years later to Captain Cook proves how wise Bougainville was.

Captain James Cook was the first European to take a sailing ship inside the Reef: that is to say to sail between the Reef and the shore. And what a terrible time he had! First his ship the *Endeavour* ran aground; its keel was sheared clean through by coral, *"as though cut by an instrument,"* and the ship had to be

beached. As soon as *Endeavour* was repaired, Cook tried again to work his way north inside the Reef. But he made slow progress. For the inshore waters were strewn with hidden reefs and rocky islands. From the masthead Cook could see that *"We were surrounded on every side with such dangers that I was at a loss which way to steer."* Eventually, he was forced to drop anchor, *"completely embayed with islands and reefs"*. Cook then made a decision which must have seemed reasonable at the time, but which led to near-disaster. Seeing a gap in the wall in the outer Reef, he decided to make for the open sea. With its ship's boat rowing cautiously ahead, *Endeavour* crept out through one of the rare gaps in the wall of coral. But Cook soon found that he had jumped out of the frying pan into the fire. All too soon winds and currents were forcing the *Endeavour* back on to the seaward wall of the Reef.

And the seaward wall of the Reef is a place of death.

"Before long," wrote Cook, *"it fell quite Calm. We sounded several times in the night,*

but found no bottom with 140 fathoms (256 metres) of line. A little after 4 o'clock, the roaring of the surf was plainly heard, and at daybreak the vast foaming breakers, towards which the Ship was being carried, were too plainly to be seen not a mile (1.6 kilometres) from us. We had not an air of wind, and there was no possibility of anchoring. In this distressed situation we had nothing but Providence and the small assistance of our boats to trust to. The yawl and the longboat were sent ahead to tow." But in spite of their efforts, "Endeavour was soon not 80 yards (73 metres) from the breakers, and the same Sea that washed the sides of the Ship rose in a breaker prodigiously high, so that between us and distruction was only a valley the breadth of one wave. We had hardly a hope of saving the Ship, or indeed our lives . . . All dangers we had escaped so far were little in comparison of being thrown upon this Reef, where the Ship must be dashed to pieces in a moment. For a Reef such as is here spoken of is scarcely known in Europe. It is a wall of Coral Rock rising almost perpendicular out of the unfathomable Ocean, and the waves meeting so sudden a resistance make a most terrible Surf, breaking great mountains high. At this critical juncture, a small air of wind sprang up, so small that at any other time we should not have observed it; and with this and the help of our boats, the ship moved off the Reef in a slanting direction. But in less than 10 Minutes, we had as flat a Calm as ever . . . Then a small opening was seen in the Reef." This was their salvation. With the boats towing, and a favourable current helping them Endeavour was swept in through the channel. "Depth 30 to 7 fathoms (54 to 12 metres)," wrote Cook, "with irregular soundings and foul bottom until we were quite within the Reef where we anchored, happy once more to encounter those shoals which a few days earlier we had been so pleased to get clear of."

Cook was arguably the greatest practical

Modern equipment makes possible the detailed exploration of the Reef's underwater world.

seaman there has ever been; if *he* got into difficulties off the Reef it is not surprising that lesser mortals frequently fell victim to it. Indeed the coral structures are littered with the wrecks of literally hundreds of sailing ships, and it wasn't until the age of steam that the Reef was properly explored. Right up to the 1960s new reefs were being discovered and old ones repositioned on navigators' charts.

The exploration of the Reef was followed by its exploitation. And in this exploitation lay the seeds of a potential tragedy.

The exploitation of the Reef has always been on a comparatively small scale. There has been none of the wanton destruction which has taken place in, say, the tropical rain forests of the world. However, *any* exploitation is a hazard, because of the Reef's extreme vulnerability to change.

The Reef is a structure of living corals. On the good health of its corals depends the good health of its 240 species of birds, its 1,500 species of fish, its 4,000 species of molluscs and its 10,000 species of sponges. If the corals die, these other creatures die too.

Corals may *look* tough; but in fact they are only able to flourish under certain restricted conditions. The temperature, the salinity and the purity of the water all have to be *exactly* right. If, for example, corals are exposed for just half an hour to fresh water, they die. If they are covered in sediment, they die. They are kept in good health by a complex ecological-system in which fish, sea-plants and corals depend on one another for survival. Take away one type of fish, one type of sea-plant or one type of coral and the whole system is in danger of collapse.

For thousands of years the exploitation of the Reef was on so small a scale that its ecological-system was not threatened. Aborigines used the Reef as a fishing-ground. But they, like many so-called primitive people, were careful husbanders of the Earth's resources. They did the Reef no harm. Nor at first did the Europeans, who in the 19th century took mother-of-pearl and corals from the reefs, and guano from the islands. But early this century one of the Reef's oldest inhabitants was hunted to near-extermination. A turtle-canning factory

was set up on Heron Island. By the early 1930s there was hardly a turtle left. The canning factory was turned into a tourist resort.

The coming of tourists posed a threat to the Reef all the more serious because it was difficult to pinpoint exactly what damage the tourists were doing. However, to quote Dr. Endean's classic work, *Australia's Great Barrier Reef:* "*The human activity which has probably had the most devastating effect on the Reef is the selective removal of elements of the fauna . . . species that occupy key positions have* (often) *been collected intensively.*" The removal of one or two of the Reef's key species upset its delicate balance. To give an example. One of the most intensively-hunted fish on the Reef is the giant groper. The giant groper feeds on starfish; in particular it feeds on *Acanthaster planci*, a type of starfish known as the Crown-of-Thorns. These Crown-of-Thorns starfish feed on corals. Once again to quote Doctor Endean, "*Acanthaster planci preys chiefly on hard corals, digesting away the flesh and leaving only the skeleton.*" So what happened was this. In parts of the Reef where there were a lot of tourists, the giant gropers were virtually exterminated. Because there were no giant gropers, there was nothing to eat the Crown-of-Thorns. So the Crown-of-Thorns multiplied and ate the corals, "*reducing vast areas of the Reef to a drab and lifeless skeleton.*"

At much the same time as the Reef was being badly damaged by the Crown-of-Thorns, it was realised it was also being threatened by other dangers. In the north, the felling of tropical rain forests had led to soil erosion; vast quantities of sediment were being washed out to sea, and this sediment was choking the coral to death. In the south, the shallow waters inside the Reef were subjected to the threat of pollution by sewage and chemicals. The granting of licences for off-shore oil exploration raised the spectre of oil pollution. Australians became aware that a unique part of their heritage was at risk.

To start with it was only a handful of scientists and a small number of diving and snorkelling enthusiasts who championed the cause of the Reef. However, during the 1960s the Great

Barrier Reef Committee led a campaign to exercise limited control over the way the Reef was exploited; and this led to a growing awareness of the issues involved. Australians in general, and young Australians in particular, began to demand that their heritage was protected. This led the federal government, in 1975, to pass the Great Barrier Reef Marine Park Act, the main provision of which was *"the establishment, control, care and development of a marine park"*. In fact two marine parks were created: the Capricornia (12,000 square km) in the south, and the Cairns (34,000 square km) in the north. Conservationists regarded this as no more than a first step in the right direction; the government of Queensland, however, was anxious to exploit the Reef's resources, and cried "Enough!" For awhile there was direct confrontation between those who wished to conserve the Reef and those who wished to exploit it. However, this gave

Drilling for natural gas takes place at many points off Australia's coastline.

way gradually to the realisation that both conserving *and* developing were called for, and that the two must somehow be made compatible. In an effort to satisfy both needs, the Reef was divided into a number of "buffer zones", each zone with its quota of permissible uses. "Use not abuse" became the slogan of the 1970s.

In recent years, as more and more people have become aware of the Reef's unique and fragile beauty, there has been a growing insistence that it should be properly cared for. In 1981 it was added to UNESCO's World Heritage list; and in 1983 the area of its marine parks was dramatically increased to include virtually all reefs between Torres Strait and the Tropic of Capricorn.

Today the Great Barrier Reef's Marine Park covers more than 340,000 square km, which makes it by far the largest conservation-area on Earth. The story of how this unique and wonderful part of our heritage has been preserved, is a story of which Australians can be proud.

Index

Suggestions for Further Reading

Acknowledgements

Béchervaise, John. *Australia: World of Difference,* 1967

Cameron, Ian. *To the Farthest Ends of the Earth,* 1980

Feeken, E., Feeken G, and Spate O.H.K. *The Discovery and Exploration of Australia,* 1970

Endean, Robert. *Australia's Great Barrier Reef,* 1982

Lamprell, Bernard. *Sea Explorers of Australia,* 1978

Laseron, Charles. *Ancient Australia,* 1969 (revised edition)

Lockwood Douglas. *We, the Aborigines,* 1963

Macmillan Australian Atlas, 1983

McGregor, C and the Editors of Time-Life Books. *The Great Barrier Reef,* 1974

Moffitt, I and the Editors of Time-Life Books. *The Australian Outback,* 1976

Moorehead, Alan. *Cooper's Creek,* 1963

Simpson, Colin. *Adam in Ochre*

Illustrations which appear in this book are from the following sources:
National Library of Australia: page 13.
Government of Western Australia: page 9 (bottom).
South Australian Government: pages 40, 42.
British Museum (Natural History): page 29 (top).
Mansell Collection: pages 36, 38, 39.
National Maritime Museum: pages 18, 21, 22, 32.
State Library of Victoria: page 37.
Agent General for Queensland: pages 54, 55, 56, 57.
Australian Information Service: pages 11, 16, 20, 25, 52, 53, 59 and Back Cover.
Australian Tourist Commission: Front Cover , End papers, pages 10, 14, 24, 27, 29 (bottom), 31, 44, 46, 50, 54.

All other illustrations are drawn from the Royal Geographical Society's library and archives. Those appearing on pages 15, 19, 24, 27, 30, 33, 35, 44, 46 and 47 were specially photographed by Robert Glen.

The extract from *Cooper's Creek* on page 40 is quoted by permission of the Estate of Alan Moorehead.

Special thanks are due to David Wileman and Francis Herbert at the Royal Geographical Society and to Melita Webster of the Australian High Commission, London. Their research assistance has proved invaluable.

LONGMAN GROUP LIMITED
Longman House
Burnt Mill, Harlow, Essex CM20 2JE, England
and Associated Companies throughout the World

This book was co-ordinated by Michael Nyman and produced by Pamino Publications, 58/60 Kensington Church St., London W8.

Text © Donald Payne 1985

This edition © Pamino Publications 1985

First published 1985
ISBN 0 582 39288 8

Cameron, Ian, *1924–*
    Exploring Australia.——(Royal Geographical Society exploring series)
    1. Australia——Discovery and exploration
    Rn: Donald Gordon Payne I. Title II. Series
    919.4'04   DU97

    ISBN 0–582–39288–8

Designed by Jim Reader
Production services by Book Production Consultants, Cambridge

Printed in Great Britain by Blantyre Printing & Binding Co. Ltd., Glasgow